Art and Civilization

Other titles in the series
Art and Civilization:

Prehistory
Ancient Egypt
Ancient Greece
Ancient Rome
The Medieval World

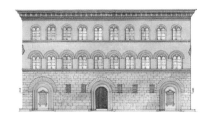

The Renaissance

Rupert Matthews

Illustrations by Paola Ravaglia, Alessandro Cantucci,
Fabiano Fabbrucci, Andrea Morandi, Lorenzo Cecchi

PETER BEDRICK BOOKS

NEW YORK

Published in the United States in 2000
by PETER BEDRICK BOOKS
A division of NTC/Contemporary Publishing Group, Inc.
4255 West Touhy Avenue, Lincolnwood (Chicago), Illinois
60646-1975 U.S.A.
Library of Congress Cataloging-in-Publication CIP data
is available from the United States Library of Congress

The Renaissance was created and produced by
McRae Books Srl, via de' Rustici, 5 – Florence (Italy)
e-mail: mcrae@tin.it

Text: Rupert Matthews
Main illustrations: Paola Ravaglia, Studio Stalio (Alessandro Cantucci,
Fabiano Fabbrucci, Andrea Morandi), Lorenzo Cecchi
Other illustrations: Gian paolo Faleschini, Antonella Pastorelli
Picture research: Erika Barrow
Graphic Design: Marco Nardi, Anne McRae
Editing: Ronne Randall
Layout and cutouts: Ornella Fassio, Adriano Nardi
Color separations: Fotolito Toscana, Florence and Litocolor, Florence

Printed in Italy by Giunti Industrie Grafiche Spa, Prato
International Standard Book Number: 0-87226-618-4

99 00 01 02 03 15 14 13 12 11 10 9 8 7 6 5 4 3 2

Contents

David, *a statue carved by Michelangelo in 1501–4, shows the strong influence of ancient Greek statues.*

Portrait by Piero della Francesca of Federico da Montefeltro, Duke of Urbino. Federico was one of many powerful princes who ruled in Italy during the Renaissance. They controlled large armies and commissioned many of the most important new buildings and works of art.

Introduction

For two hundred years from around 1400 on, Europe was transformed by a flood of new ideas. There were new ways of building, a new style of art and new ways of living. The arts were changed by a desire to show the world as it really was, not merely in symbolic terms. Paintings and sculptures began to show real people in real places for the first time since the Classical period. As Europe recovered from the terrible plague which had killed off almost one-third of its population in the 14th century, there was strong economic growth and a surge in trade and exchange of every kind. In this new atmosphere many people gained a stronger sense of themselves as individuals and became aware of their own worth. In religion this new feeling led to a demand for reform which tore the Christian Church apart, but at the same time strengthened religious feeling. This period of history and the artistic and intellectual changes it brought is known as the Renaissance, a word which means "rebirth."

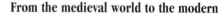

A drawing by Leonardo da Vinci, showing a glider. Leonardo, an artist and an inventor, introduced modern technical drawing.

The ideal Renaissance Man

During the Renaissance it was believed that the ideal man would be interested in everything. The artist Leonardo da Vinci (1452–1519) is the best example of this new ideal. Born in the small town of Vinci, near Florence, Leonardo trained as a painter under the Florentine artist Verrocchio. His mastery of light and shade and ability to put real character into his paintings soon made him a famous painter. But Leonardo was also an accomplished musician, sculptor, scientist and architect. He designed instruments of war, fortifications, waterways and machines of all types (including the bat like glider shown above), although most were never built. Leonardo also studied plants, animals and people, producing detailed drawings of them all. Leonardo is one of the few artists whose reputation as a genius has remained intact since his death to the present day.

A drawing by Leonardo da Vinci, generally thought to be a self-portrait.

From the medieval world to the modern

Before the Renaissance, many Europeans thought that the world was a large flat disk, surrounded by a giant sphere on which were fixed the sun, stars and planets. During the Renaissance these ideas were first questioned, then overthrown. In 1522 a Spanish ship returned after sailing completely around the world, proving the earth was round. A few people began to think that the earth went around the sun, not the sun around the earth. It began to seem that humans were not the center of God's creation, but just a small part of the universe.

A globe made by Martin Behaim of Nuremburg in 1492. It only shows Europe, Africa and Asia. European explorers visited America for the first time that same year.

The School of Athens, *painted in about 1510 by Raphael (1483–1520), decorates a room in the Vatican in Rome. The large fresco is opposite a painting showing learned churchmen discussing the Holy Trinity. The two paintings showed how ancient learning and Christianity could exist side by side.*

The School of Athens

This famous fresco by Raphael shows an imaginary scene with the great thinkers of ancient Greece gathered together in a single school. The building is based on a design by the architect Donato Bramante (1444–1514). Many of the figures are represented by portraits of well-known Renaissance people. At the center of the picture are Plato (portrait of Leonardo) (1), with his book *Timaeus*, and Aristotle (2), with his book *Nicomachean Ethics*. To the left of the main figures are the soldier Alcibiades (3), in armor, talking to the historian Xenophon (4) and a snub-nosed Socrates (5). The philosopher Epicurus (6) is shown on the far left wearing a wreath of leaves and writing his books on the value of a simple life. To the right sits Pythagoras (7) noting down his harmonic scale. In the central foreground Heraclitus (portrait of Michelangelo) (8) leans on a block of stone. The figure sprawled on the steps is Diogenes the Cynic (9). In the foreground on the right, holding a divider is Euclid (portrait of Bramante) (10) teaching geometry, and wearing the crown is Ptolemy (11) discussing astronomy with Zoroaster (12). Raphael (13) himself is the young man on the extreme right wearing a black hat.

From left to right, portraits of Italian humanists Pico della Mirandola (1463–94), Marsilio Ficino (1433–99), Angelo Poliziano (1454–94), Gentile de Becchi and Cristoforo Landino.

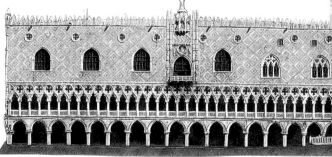

Humanists

During the early Renaissance, scholars began studying the works of ancient Latin and Greek writers, particularly Cicero and Plato. They discovered a philosophy of life quite different from that of the medieval Christian Church. By trying to merge the two teachings, the scholars created humanism. They believed that individuals could develop their own lives for good or evil and could control their own destiny. Humanists became aware that the various copies of ancient texts differed from each other due to mistakes made in centuries of copying. They tried to rediscover the original texts by comparing the different versions. Later humanists applied these techniques to the Bible, with dramatic results.

These ballot bags, each carrying the symbol of a ward, were used in Florence for city elections. Like many Italian cities, Florence was divided into areas called wards, each of which had its own badge. Each ward elected one person to represent it on the city council and had to raise a certain number of men for the city army, pay a set amount of tax to the city government and administer justice in its area.

Italian city-states

During the Renaissance Italy was divided into about 30 different states. Some, such as the Kingdom of Naples and the Papal States, were large and powerful, but most were small city-states. During the early Renaissance city-states were democracies in which wealthy male citizens elected their government. The cities fought many wars and were always trying to outdo each other with beautiful buildings or works of art. It was against this political background of rivalry, competition and intrigue that the Renaissance began.

The Town Hall in Siena, a small republic in Tuscany. From some 5,000 citizens, Siena elected 860 part-time officials as well as the town council headed by the Captain of the People. A high proportion of the people in Siena were entitled to vote.

The Doge's Palace in Venice. The Venetian elected a Doge, who held wide-ranging political power for life, as well as a town council. Fewer people in Venice had the vote than in most other city-states.

A miniature showing Constantinople. Known as Byzantium before the Middle Ages, the ancient capital of the eastern Roman Empire preserved much of the knowledge of Greece and Rome that was rediscovered by Renaissance scholars.

In 1338–9 Ambrogio Lorenzetti (c. 1300–48) painted a mural in the Town Hall of Siena which showed the benefits of good and bad city government. Good government included industry, education, good housing, order and honest trade.

Medieval poet Dante Alighieri (1265–1321) studied ancient Latin texts, reinterpreting them in his works. He, and other poets such as Petrarch and Boccaccio, set the foundations for the Renaissance.

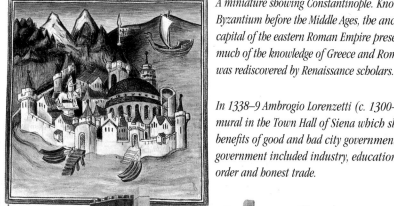

St. Jerome

St Jerome (c. 342–420) in his study (1) was a favorite subject for Renaissance artists. They admired the saint, who had studied science, religion, art and philosophy. Born in the town of Stridon, Jerome studied Greek and Roman philosophy in Rome before traveling to Antioch and Bethlehem. Here he gathered together various early Christian writings and produced the basis for the Bible as we know it today. Renaissance artists portrayed him in a study packed with books and scientific equipment in order to encourage men to follow his example.

One of the greatest humanist scholars was Erasmus (c. 1466–1536). Born in Rotterdam, he joined a monastery near Gouda. But in the 1490s he left the monastery to teach at the universities of Paris, Oxford and Cambridge. He wrote several books praising humanist ideas and condemned the corruption and inflexible teachings of the Catholic Church. However, he opposed reformers such as Luther, whom he saw as dividing Christian people rather than reforming the Church. Respected by all sides in the religious and humanist disputes of the early 16th century, Erasmus lived his final years in Switzerland.

Sir Thomas More (1478–1535) was an English lawyer and politician who became a leading humanist scholar. He learned much from Erasmus and worked hard to end the worst abuses within the Church in England. He failed, however, and in 1534 King Henry VIII broke the English Church away from Rome. More refused to accept the split and Henry had him executed for treason. More thus became a martyr to the Catholic Church he had tried to reform and was made a saint.

The pathway to knowledge, a design set into the paving of Siena Cathedral.

he path to knowledge

uring the Renaissance education
as highly valued. Most towns had
hools in which wealthy children
arned to read and write. Every city had
s own university, and the lessons were
pen to everyone who had the time to attend.
eachers passed on their knowledge, and encouraged
udents to ask questions and debate the issues.

Guilds, Merchants and Trade

During the Renaissance a major change swept across Europe. For centuries the chief source of wealth had been land and the crops grown on it. But from about 1400 on wealth began to be concentrated in manufacturing and trade. Guilds were set up in towns to control the quality and price of goods, while merchants organized the transporting of goods and products between cities and countries. Soon some merchants began acting as bankers. They lent money to traders and rulers to be paid back with interest over a period of time. By about 1450 an early form of capitalist economy had grown up in Italy. Within 50 years the system had spread throughout Europe. There seemed no limit to the wealth which could be generated.

Weavers dyeing silk. Italians learned how to ra[i]se silkworms from the Chinese in about 1300 and so[on] dominated the European trade in this luxury fabr[ic].

The coat of arms of the stone masons and wood carvers guild of Florence.

A carpenter at work in his workshop while his wife spins in the background. Many families practiced more than one trade at a time.

Skilled craftsmen

The trade in textiles was vital to the growth of trade and wealth in early Renaissance Italy. By 1400 Italian weavers dominated the wool trade, the weavers of Florence buying their wool from as far afield as England and selling cloth at fairs in Germany and France. Italian merchants set up businesses not only in Europe, but also in North Africa, in the Ottoman Empire and deep into Asia.

Left: The symbols of the various trade guilds in Florence. 1. Tailors, 2. Goldsmiths, 3. Peasants, 4. Vasemakers, 5. Bakers, 6. Butchers, 7. Wine sellers, 8. Launderers, 9. Barbers, 10. Carpenters. In most cities the guilds were made up of all the men who practiced a certain trade, such as weaving, carpentry or medicine. The guilds made sure that only qualified men could carry out the trade, and they often set prices and wages as well. In some cities, such as Padua, the guilds took part in city government and administration. They collected the taxes among their members and paid for soldiers in time of war.

The Money Changer and His Wife

This painting by Quentin Massys (1466–1530) shows a money changer (1) carefully weighing coins to make sure valuable metal has not been clipped from the edges. His wife (2), leafing through a religious book, looks on. Money changers had books of coin designs to identify coins from distant lands and tables which showed how pure the gold and silver was in coins from different countries.

The Florentine
florin (top) and Venetian ducat
(above) were so trusted by
merchants that other nations began
issuing coins of identical value.
Britain continued minting florins
until the 1970s.

Many merchants carried
delicate scales in special
pocket pouches. They were
used to weigh coins to
determine their value.

A shop selling cloth

During the Renaissance families who gained their wealth
from trade became richer than old noble families whose wealth
came from the land. The nobles often tried to snub the
merchants by passing sumptuary laws, which declared that only
noblemen could wear furs, silks and other luxury fabrics. But the
merchants soon acquired political power themselves and most
sumptuary laws were abolished.

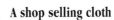

Lorenzo de' Medici, "the Magnificent"
(1449–92), a banker in Florence who
used his wealth and power to dominate
the government of the city. In the 16th
century the Medici family became
dukes and took over the city
government completely.

Trade routes in 1500

By the year 1500 merchants had set up regular trade routes across Europe and the Mediterranean. Major cities had agents working for foreign merchants and places where visiting traders could stay and their goods be stored in safety.

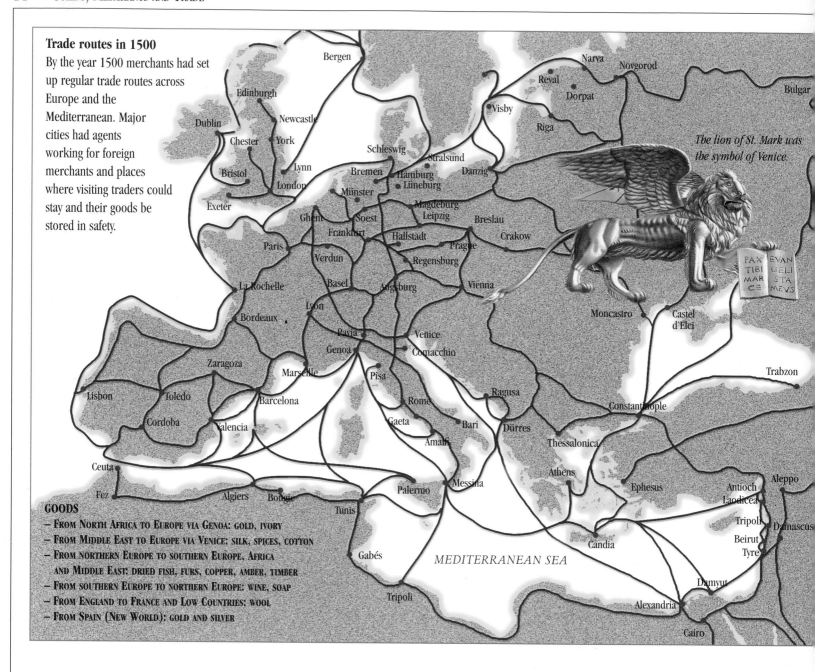

The lion of St. Mark was the symbol of Venice.

PAX TIBI MAR CE EVAN GELI STA MEVS

MEDITERRANEAN SEA

GOODS

– FROM NORTH AFRICA TO EUROPE VIA GENOA: GOLD, IVORY
– FROM MIDDLE EAST TO EUROPE VIA VENICE: SILK, SPICES, COTTON
– FROM NORTHERN EUROPE TO SOUTHERN EUROPE, AFRICA AND MIDDLE EAST: DRIED FISH, FURS, COPPER, AMBER, TIMBER
– FROM SOUTHERN EUROPE TO NORTHERN EUROPE: WINE, SOAP
– FROM ENGLAND TO FRANCE AND LOW COUNTRIES: WOOL
– FROM SPAIN (NEW WORLD): GOLD AND SILVER

Bruges and the north

Many rich merchants built luxurious palaces in the burgeoning cities. These generally had shops and warehouses at street level where they could carry on their businesses. The second floor housed the main reception rooms and the private apartments of the most important members of the family. The upper floors, reached by long staircases and generally hotter in summer and cooler in winter, were reserved for children, less important family members and servants. The basic plan for this kind of palace (very similar to the ones in use in ancient Rome over 1,000 years before) came from Florence and gradually spread to other parts of Europe.

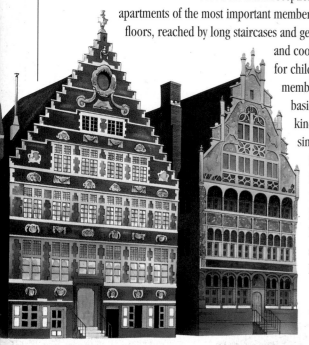

The Hanseatic League

From about 1350 on several cities in northern Germany formed the Hanseatic League. This organization had warships and armies to protect its merchants as they traveled from Britain and France deep into Russia and eastern Europe. They traded raw materials from the east for manufactured goods from the west. The League met in Lübeck and its formal documents were marked by a seal which showed a small merchant ship, or cog. After about 1450 the Hanseatic League declined in importance as Dutch and English merchants became more active.

The seal of the city of Kiel, on the north German coast, shows a typical Hanseatic trading ship.

Venice

Venice was the second largest city in Italy, with about 120,000 inhabitants. It had a large navy and hundreds of merchant ship which dominated the sea routes of the Mediterranea Venetian trading ships plie the Mediterranean and eve ventured out into the Atlantic to reach London and Bruges. During the 14 century Venetian merchant controlled the very lucrativ spice, silk and perfume routes between Europe an the Far East. The city became fabulously wealthy at this time.

*ow: This beautiful fresco shows a lively scene during the
building of the Hospital of Santa Maria della Scala in the
ntral Italian city of Siena. It is part of a "cycle" (group of
ated works) of eight paintings showing events during the
spital's history. The paintings were done in the main hall
the Hospital on the ground floor, an area that was
obably used as a men's dormitory.*

*The layout for the Italian city of Palma Nova betrays
the violence of the era. The city is surrounded by
a wide moat and is protect by bastions on
which cannon can be mounted. The streets of
the city run to the city walls so that troops
can be rushed to any point of danger.*

*An allegorical illustration of how
a city can be likened to
the human body. The
head is like the
government, providing
instructions, while the heart
is likened to the Church,
which provides
compassion and
morality. The limbs
are likened to
defensive
towers.*

This view of an imaginary ideal city was painted in about 1450, probably for the Duke of Urbino. During the Renaissance, the narrow medieval streets of many cities were replaced by wide piazzas and elegant streets. Urbino was largely rebuilt by Duke Federico in the later 16th century.

The beautiful Santa Trinita Bridge in Florence was bu[ilt] in 1567 to a design by Michelangelo, who based [its] elegant arches on elliptical curves. The statues we[re] added to celebrate the marriage of Cosimo II de' Medic[i's] wedding in 1608. The bridge was blown up in 1944 by [the] retreating German army, but has been carefully restore[d.]

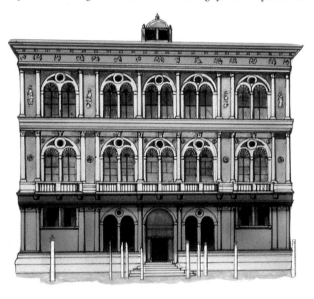

The Palazzo Vendramin in Venice is one of several early Renaissance palaces in the city. As with many such palaces, the building was later abandoned by the family that built it and divided into apartments and rented out. The arched windows are typical of Venetian structures of the period.

The round Tempietto was built in 1502 by Don[ato] Bramante (1444–1514) and is considered the first pu[re] Renaissance building in Rome. Bramante blended ancie[nt] Roman styles with 16th-century designs to create th[e] chapel. It was built to mark the spot where St. Pet[er] was crucified, its elegant proportions matchi[ng] the small space availab[le.]

The Gothic church of Santa Maria Novella in Florence was built by the Dominican monks in the 14th century, but the top part of the façade was added in 1470 by Leon Battista Alberti in pure Renaissance style. The work was paid for by the Rucellai family, who grew enormously wealthy by developing a special red dye for woolen cloth. Their symbol appears several times on the façade.

Brunelleschi, the architect of Florence Cathedral's celebrated dome, also designed Florence's beautiful Ospedale degli Innocenti.

Ancient architecture and new architecture

In 1452 Leon Battista Alberti (1404–72) from Genoa produced a massive, 10-volum[e] work on architecture, *De Re Aedificatoria*. Alberti emphasized the elegance of ancient Roman architecture and included detailed drawings of columns, capital[s] pediments and other details from ancient ruins. The book was very influential and persuaded many architects to adopt the styles of ancient Rome.

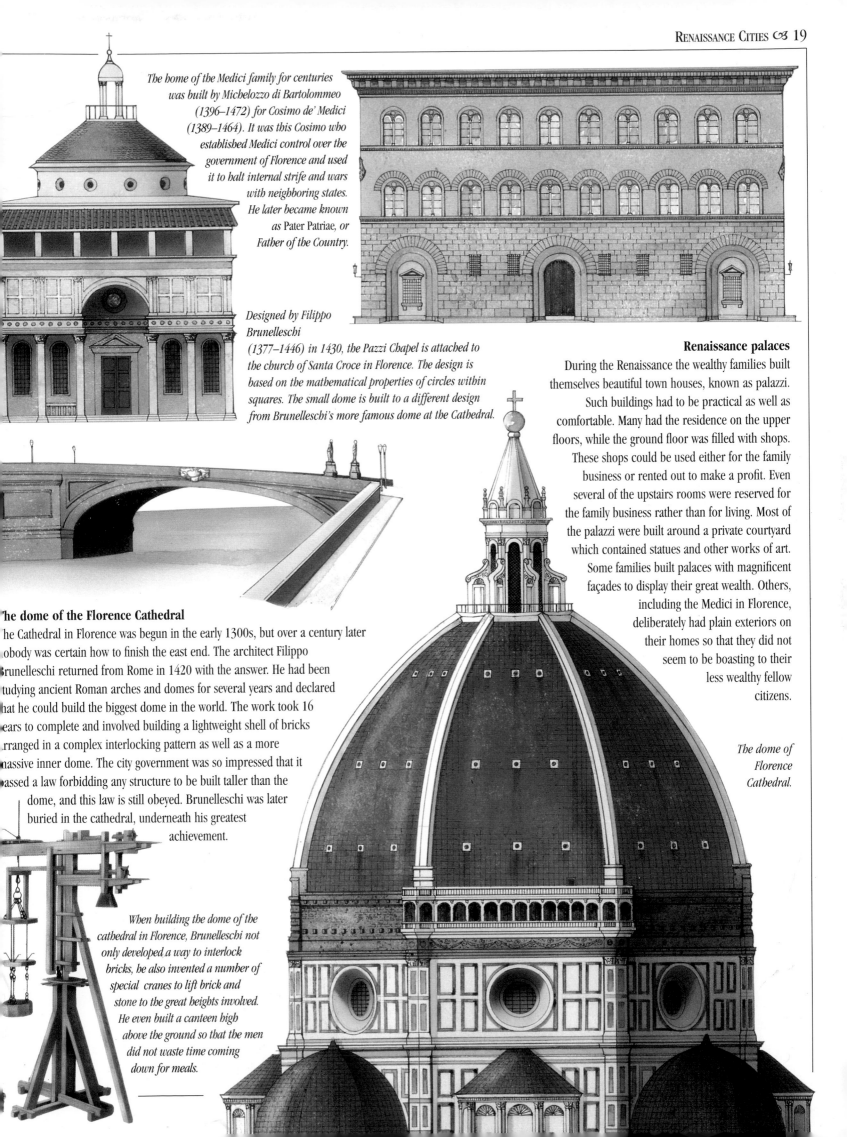

The home of the Medici family for centuries was built by Michelozzo di Bartolommeo (1396–1472) for Cosimo de' Medici (1389–1464). It was this Cosimo who established Medici control over the government of Florence and used it to halt internal strife and wars with neighboring states. He later became known as Pater Patriae, or Father of the Country.

Designed by Filippo Brunelleschi (1377–1446) in 1430, the Pazzi Chapel is attached to the church of Santa Croce in Florence. The design is based on the mathematical properties of circles within squares. The small dome is built to a different design from Brunelleschi's more famous dome at the Cathedral.

Renaissance palaces

During the Renaissance the wealthy families built themselves beautiful town houses, known as palazzi. Such buildings had to be practical as well as comfortable. Many had the residence on the upper floors, while the ground floor was filled with shops. These shops could be used either for the family business or rented out to make a profit. Even several of the upstairs rooms were reserved for the family business rather than for living. Most of the palazzi were built around a private courtyard which contained statues and other works of art. Some families built palaces with magnificent façades to display their great wealth. Others, including the Medici in Florence, deliberately had plain exteriors on their homes so that they did not seem to be boasting to their less wealthy fellow citizens.

The dome of Florence Cathedral.

The dome of the Florence Cathedral

The Cathedral in Florence was begun in the early 1300s, but over a century later nobody was certain how to finish the east end. The architect Filippo Brunelleschi returned from Rome in 1420 with the answer. He had been studying ancient Roman arches and domes for several years and declared that he could build the biggest dome in the world. The work took 16 years to complete and involved building a lightweight shell of bricks arranged in a complex interlocking pattern as well as a more massive inner dome. The city government was so impressed that it passed a law forbidding any structure to be built taller than the dome, and this law is still obeyed. Brunelleschi was later buried in the cathedral, underneath his greatest achievement.

When building the dome of the cathedral in Florence, Brunelleschi not only developed a way to interlock bricks, he also invented a number of special cranes to lift brick and stone to the great heights involved. He even built a canteen high above the ground so that the men did not waste time coming down for meals.

Private Life

A game of chess being enjoyed by Margaret of Angoulême (1492–1549), one of the most educated women of the Renaissance. In addition to helping artists, she encouraged humanist scholars and promoted new methods of agriculture.

Daily life changed dramatically during the Renaissance. The most obvious change was that the concept of a private life began to have meaning in Europe. During the Middle Ages there was little privacy, even for the rich. All the members of a family would live and sleep together in the same room. In castles or towns several different families might share a large hall, separated only by curtains. By the early 15th century, however, it was becoming normal for each family to have its own house or apartment. For people with even small amounts of money houses had a number of small bedrooms for the different sexes. Modesty and privacy were introduced to society, together with an awareness of morality. The increase in trade allowed ideas to spread quickly, so that fashions in clothing and furniture could change more rapidly than before. As more people became wealthy they began to have leisure time away from work. Personal hygiene became increasingly important and serious efforts were made in most cities to improve sewage and refuse systems.

This woman wears a h[...] made from rolled cloth. Ne[...] dyes and manufacturi[...] techniques meant that cloth[...] could be replaced more eas[...] with new, fashionable iten[...]

Venetian glas[s]

During the Renaissance Venetia[n] glassblowers rediscovered t[he] skills of making fine glass. This gobl[et] was made in about 1475 on t[he] Venetian island of Murano and [is] one of the earliest examples [of] enameled and gilded decoration on [a] small glass. Such beautif[ul] pieces were for the ric[h] but even middlecla[ss] families could afford le[ss] ornate glas[s]

Indoor entertainment

For the first time people other than the nobility began to have time to spend on leisure, not just on work. These hours could be filled with games, music, drinking or study. Even fairly modest households contained musical instruments, game tables and other leisure equipment.

This traveling games box of the 15th century includes boards for chess, roulette, fox and geese and nine men's morris. The outside of the box has a board for backgammon.

A group of musicians: the man is playing a lute, while next to him stands a woman playing a recorder. The keyboard instrument is a virginal, and the woman on the right is playing a viol.

Renaissance music

During the Renaissance music began to be played for sheer enjoyment, instead of only as part of religious services. Printed music sheets and instruction books led to the spread of popular chamber music. Beautiful music was enjoyed in many private homes.

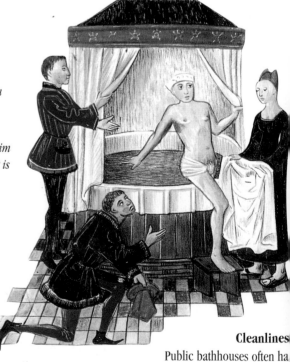

Cleanlines[s]

Public bathhouses often ha[d] bad reputations, but rich people could afford a private bath[.] Renaissance people were more hygienic and clean than [is] generally recognized and the wealthy enjoyed frequent baths[.]

en's clothing

en's fashion could be very elaborate.
rocaded silks, velvets and plush woolens
came common, and the abundance of
eats, capes and cloaks made for sumptuous
splays. Even famous artists, such as
ichelangelo, were known to design clothes.

Fashion varied widely from country to country. This 15th-century Italian man wears a flowing, pleated cape and richly decorated stockings.

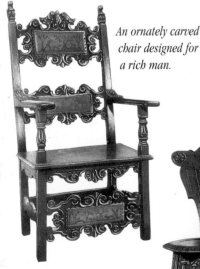

An ornately carved chair designed for a rich man.

A small chair without arms allowing the large dresses worn by women to be draped over the sides.

The Arnolfini Marriage

In 1434 the Flemish painter Jan van Eyck (c. 1389–1441) painted the wedding of Italian merchant Giovanni Arnolfini (1) to Giovanna Cenami (2). The painting is full of symbolism, such as the dog (3) for faithfulness, the oranges (4) for fruitfulness and the double bed (5) for marriage itself. However, some symbols, such as the chandelier with only one candle (6), are more obscure. The mirror (7) shows the couple from behind with the witnesses standing in the spot from which the scene is viewed. Van Eyck perfected a method of mixing and applying oil paints which his pupil Petrus Christus took to Italy where it was used by all the later Renaissance artists.

Middleclass families

This domestic portrait, painted in 1586, shows a family from Bruges, hands pressed humbly together as they say grace, settling down to eat. While the roast meat (1) and bread (2) make up a simple meal, the rich silver and pewter tableware (3) and the presence of a maid (4) show that the family is well-to-do. Their dark, sober clothing is typical of the new Protestant middle classes. It is a large family – the parents (5) are flanked to the left by five sons and to the right by three daughters.

Royalty

Although new merchant families rose to power, much of Europe continued to be ruled by old royal families. In England the Tudors, a Welsh family only distantly related to the royal family, took the throne in 1485. The wealthy banking family, the Medici, became dukes of Florence in 1537. In Milan the illegitimate, but hugely talented, mercenary Francesco Sforza became duke in 1450 after marrying the previous duke's daughter. It was a time when new families could rise to the very top.

Queen Elizabeth I (1533–1603) ruled England for 45 years. Her stiff, richly embroidered clothing was typical of royalty in the 16th century.

This terracotta plaque by Pisano shows two noble boys being taught grammar.

A scene showing a school for boys from wealthy Italian families.

Education

Education enjoyed massive growth during the Renaissance. Noblemen were no longer expected to spend their lives fighting and could afford to learn to read and then use this skill to acquire knowledge. Trade guilds often set up schools to teach accountancy, law and other skills needed by ambitious merchants. Less practical subjects included reading ancient Greek or Roman texts, grammar, and the ability to make good speeches. There was no system of examinations, even at the universities, so pupils left school when they were needed to help with the family business or when they felt they had learned enough.

...carving from 15th-century England shows ...nan removing lice from a woman's ...ir. Picking out lice by hand gave ...nporary relief, but only daily ...mbing could permanently remove ...e eggs.

Keeping clean

As cities began to grow, so did an awareness of problems caused by human waste and smells. Simply dumping garbage and excrement out the door was no longer acceptable. Instead streets were built with gutters into which waste could be placed to be flushed away by the next rain fall. It was soon realized that diseases spread where hygiene was bad, but people thought the smells were the problem and scattered perfume which had no effect.

...enaissance homes

...urban living became increasingly sophisticated, ...too did the homes in which people lived. ...Ferrara, in 1494, Duke Ercole I began ...massive rebuilding project which saw ...e construction of small, one-story ...ouses for craftsmen, apartment ...ouses for workers and palaces for ...e wealthy. As in other cities, people ...ere expected to have chamberpots ...r excrement and pots for other ...arbage which they would carry to ...esignated dumping grounds. By 1600 ...ouses and apartments were generally more ...olidly built and more hygiene than they had ...een 200 years earlier.

A 15th-century Englishman warms his hands and feet at an open fire. The invention of chimneys in the early Renaissance was a major advance in home comfort.

The head of a young boy modelled in terracotta by Luca della Robbia. The fact that rich families wanted such portraits of their young children showed a change in attitude toward childhood. As fewer children died in infancy, they began to be seen as having individual personalities and to be worthy of care and love.

Warfare and Weapons

Italian city-states spent most of the Renaissance in conflict over territory or trade routes. Spies, bribery and intrigue were usual, and open warfare was not uncommon. In theory armies were made up of the citizens of the city. Rich men were expected to serve as armored cavalrymen, poor men as infantry. In practice most cities hired mercenaries to fight their wars. In 1400 armies were made up of crossbowmen and pikemen, protected by movable shields, and heavy cavalry. By 1500 early guns, called harquebus, had replaced the crossbows, but they were not much more accurate. Battles were usually decided by cavalry charges while the infantry guarded the baggage and supplies. However, battles could be costly in terms of men and equipment, so most wars took the form of sieges of towns and cities. Defensive walls tended to be stronger than the attacking guns, therefore even small towns could hold out for long periods of time. Decisive victories were rare, and wars would drag on until one side wearied of the expense and agreed to a treaty. The small city of Siena, for instance, held out against its much larger neighbor Florence during centuries of on-and-off warfare. In the end Siena gave in to Florence following intense economic and diplomatic pressure, not a military defeat.

The ordinary infantry of the citizen militia were expected to bring their own weapons when called upon to fight. Maces were cheap, but effective, in close combat. Swords and spears might be carried by those willing to invest more money in weaponry.

Condottiere

By 1400 most citizens of Italian cities were too busy as merchants or bankers to serve the army except in emergencies. Most cities therefore hired a professional army of mercenaries by issuing an annual contract, called a *condotta*. The mercenary commander, or *condottiere*, used his men to man frontier posts and guard towns and villages. If war broke out, the condottiere fought the war using his own men. This led to very few battles. If one mercenary commander found himself at a serious disadvantage he would surrender rather than fight. This allowed him to keep his army intact so he could hire it out again. Italian troops became highly skilled at maneuvers, rapid marches and long sieges, but they lacked much experience of fighting open battles.

A breech-loading cannon of about 1550. In 1400 cannon had been large, heavy and inaccurate, but in 1448 the Milanese used guns to smash the walls of Caravaggio within weeks. Fifty years later, bronze cannon were light enough to be pulled by horses along with an army and be used on the battlefield. By the 1570s artillery was an accepted part of all armies' weaponry.

The Holy Roman Emperor Charles V shown in 1547 dressed as a heavy cavalryman of the time.

The Battle of San Romano

Fought in 1432 between Florence and Siena, the battle ended in a victory for Florence. The picture shows the heavily armored cavalry (1) which formed the most potent part of any army

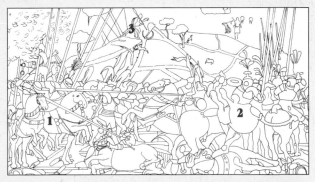

at this time. The brown horse to the right (2) is kicking backward, one of several attacking tricks a warhorse was trained to carry out on demand. Behind the cavalry are infantry (3), some armed with crossbows and others with spears and swords. In the background an infantry skirmish is shown, in an early attempt at perspective by the artist Paolo Uccello (c. 1397–1475).

Johannes Gutenberg (c. 1398–1468), the German craftsman who set up the first printing press using movable type in 1450.

Movable Type

In about 1426 Laurens Janszoon, in Haarlem, the Netherlands, had a printing press which could reproduce woodcuts a page at a time. But the crucial invention of movable type was made by Gutenberg. By using a different metal plug to print each letter it was possible to build up pages one after another from the same type instead of carving new type for each page. This made printing much cheaper and more flexible than before. Gutenberg himself used the same letters for at least three books, possibly more.

A printing workshop

Although this illustration of a printing workshop is from the early 16th century, it is almost identical to that developed by Gutenberg. On the left a man (1) stands ready with pads soaked in ink which he will pat onto the type to ink them up. In front of him a workman (2) pulls the lever to turn the screw and press the paper onto the inked type. In the right foreground a man (3) checks the final printed page for quality. Behind him a typesetter (4) arranges the individual type into a frame ready to be mounted on the printing press. The two wooden pillars (5) above the press braced it against the ceiling, making the press very rigid and strong.

Chinese printing

Printing was originally invented by the Chinese. The earliest known book was printed on May 11, 868 by a man called Wang Chieh. The book is made up of seven sheets, six of text and one of illustration, and consists of Buddhist holy scriptures. The woodcut printing is fairly sophisticated, so it is likely that printing had been invented some years earlier. The idea of printing was probably carried to Europe by merchants in the late 14th century.

Luxury books were beautifully illustrated. An effort was made to make them look as much like hand-copied manuscripts as possible.

The Printing Revolution

The key invention of the Renaissance was printing. Developed in Germany in the mid-15th century, the use of printing quickly spread across Europe, reaching Florence and Naples by 1470 and Britain and Poland a few years later. Instead of laboriously copying books by hand one at a time, a printer could turn out dozens of copies in a few days for a fraction of the cost. At first the new books tended to be religious – Bibles, hymn books or theological texts. But soon engineers were printing technical books and merchants were buying guidebooks telling them how to reach distant markets to sell their goods. Before long architects, painters and people in other professions were rushing to print their latest discoveries and ideas. The new, relatively cheap books spread these ideas across Europe with remarkable speed. This allowed developments to take place much more quickly than before, when one new idea could have taken decades to cross Europe. The ferment of ideas and the revolution in thought which came with the Renaissance would have been impossible without the printing press.

This illustration shows that during the Renaissance, more and more women were educated and able to read. The flood of relatively cheap books made it possible for modestly wealthy families to acquire extensive libraries of books. These were often translations of ancient Greek or Roman histories, but by 1550 stories of foreign travel and wonderful adventures were being printed to be read for fun.

The basic printing press consisted of a flat bed on which was mounted a frame containing the metal type. The sheet of paper was put on top of this and covered by fabric set in a second frame to act as padding. The bed was then slid under the press. When the lever was pulled, the press squeezed the paper against the inked type frame, transferring the ink from type to paper.

Printing pictures

Medieval books, copied by hand, were often beautifully decorated with hand-painted pictures embellished with gold leaf. The early printers tried to decorate their books to make them look as much like hand-copied books as possible. The first illustrations were carved by artists and were formed by ridges of wood rising from a wooden block. After printing, these black-and-white images could be colored by hand. It was found, however, that these wooden blocks quickly wore out. It soon became common for a printing workshop to have one artist who drew the original picture and a team of craftsmen who carved several copies onto wooden blocks which would last for the entire print run. This system was to last until methods of etching metal plates were developed in the 19th century.

A page from the Gutenberg Bible. Printed by Johannes Gutenberg in Mainz between 1451 and 1456, this book is the earliest known printed Bible. The book had a total of 643 sheets of paper, which were bound by hand into either one or two volumes. Although Gutenberg printed many copies, only 48 have survived to the present day.

The Reformation

During the later Renaissance the world of Christianity was torn apart by a conflict which led to intellectual debate and bloodshed on a grand scale. By about 1500 the Bible and holy writings were being printed and widely read by educated people. At the same time many people were beginning to believe that the Catholic Church was riddled with corruption, peopled by clergy who did not follow their own rules and harbored a widespread contempt for the very people the Church was meant to serve. In Germany a priest named Martin Luther was so outraged by the sale of indulgences that he began to think deeply about the Church. In 1517 he began preaching a new reformed faith which demanded a break with Roman practices and a return to the teachings of Holy Scripture. The ideas were discussed across Europe. In some areas they were taken up, in others they were rejected.

When the Holy Roman Emperor ordered his subjects to obey the Pope the reformers protested, gaining the name of Protestants. By 1540 Europe was divided between the two forms of Christianity, and war soon followed.

Henry VIII (1491–1547) was king of England from 1509. Despite his early condemnation of Martin Luther, Henry broke with the Catholic Church in 1534 when Pope Clement VII refused to annul Henry's marriage. The king later closed the monasteries, crushed a Catholic rebellion and had his son and heir educated as a Protestant.

Paul III became Pope in 1534 and, appalled by the split in Christendom caused by the Protestant movement, set out to reform the Church. He cut the size and extravagance of the Sacred College in Rome, reformed the religious orders and fought corruption. He clearly defined dogma and reasserted papal authority. Paul greatly encouraged learning and the arts in Rome and within the Church. However, he had a habit of appointing friends and family to important posts, including making his 14-year-old grandson a cardinal, which alienated some reformers.

Most people who took holy orders to become monks, nuns or priests did so for religious motives, but a few saw the move as the route to a prosperous career. Ignoring vows of poverty or chastity, such clergy indulged in singing, drinking and other sins. This painting shows a typical view of these worldly clergy indulging in unholy activities.

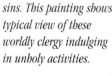

In 1534 Luther published a copy of the Bible in German, a revolutionary step, as earlier Bibles had been printed in Latin. This move enabled ordinary people to read God's word and removed a key power of the clergy.

Indulgences

In 1516 Pope Leo X decided to raise money in a manner which was to spark the Reformation. In Catholic teaching, the time a person's soul spent in Purgatory could be reduced by repentance and good works on earth. These works were recognized in a Church document called an indulgence. Leo decided that giving money to the Church to pay for the new St. Peter's Cathedral, and his own luxuries, would count as a good work. In effect this meant an indulgence would be handed over in return for cash. In 1517, the monk John Tetzel (c. 1465–1519) arrived in Saxony to sell the indulgences. There he met Martin Luther (1483–1546), who was so appalled by the sale that he drew up 95 Theses about indulgences and nailed them to the local church door, thus starting the Reformation.

The Reformers

The Reformation movement spread quickly, both within Germany and abroad. Many of the new reformers differed from Luther in their opinions of what should be done about corruption in the Church and on theological questions. New offshoot movements soon appeared. Huldrych Zwingli began a movement in Zurich, Switzerland, which in turn fostered more radical groups, including the Anabaptists. A French lawyer named John Calvin began another important form of Protestantism, which became known as Calvinism. The illustration above shows Martin Luther with some of the most important Protestant reformers.

Protestant and Catholic clergy

This hand-colored woodcut was produced in about 1545 by the artist Lucas Cranach the Elder (1472–1553). Cranach was a town official in Wittenberg and a close friend of Martin Luther. The picture sets out to portray the purity of the Protestant clergy (1), shown preaching truth to the lamb of God (2), through Christ (3) to God himself (4). Nearby holy communion (5) and baptism (6) are being properly carried out. This is contrasted to the Catholic preacher (7), shown with a demon (8) pumping ideas into his ear, who overlooks the Pope (9) counting money at a table loaded with indulgences, a monk (10) with gambling cards falling from his sleeve and other clergy carrying out dishonest or improper acts.

Science and Invention

During the Renaissance the view people had of the world changed dramatically. Until about 1400 most people believed that God created the world exactly as described in the Bible and that the writings of early Christians described all animals, plant and minerals. But as more ancient Greek and Roman writings came to light it became clear that large amounts of learning already existed. Ancient thinkers often emphasized the need to carry out experiments to test if theories were true or not, a new and exciting idea for Renaissance scholars. Soon scientists all over Europe were busily carrying out experiments in medicine, chemistry, physics, astronomy and geology. Some thought these experiments would show a divine plan for the world, others that they would give control over mystic and magical powers. At first the Catholic Church welcomed these new ideas, but by the 1540s they condemned any ideas which did not agree with the Bible. Several scientists were put in prison as a result of their ideas. In Protestant countries, however, science continued to thrive and expand.

A sketch made by Leonardo da Vinci (1452–1519) of the proportions of the human body. Leonardo was fascinated by the human body and made hundreds of sketches like this.

Learning from Experiment

Many scientists believed they could learn about the world by experimenting with real objects instead of discussing abstract theories. The chemist Theophrastus von Hohenheim, known as Paracelsus (1493–1541), spent 14 years wandering around Europe to gather information. He then settled in Basel, Switzerland, and undertook many experiments with metals, laying the foundations for later chemical research techniques. Ambroise Paré (1509–90) was the chief surgeon to the French army. He tried out new ideas in dealing with wounds, including the technique of sewing them up rather than cauterizing them with a red-hot iron. However, his theory did not match his practical skill since he believed demons caused infections and suggested prayers as a cure. Not all investigators were appreciated. Vesalius found himself condemned to death by the Catholic Church for bodysnatching and only escaped by going on the hazardous pilgrimage to Jerusalem, though he died on his way back.

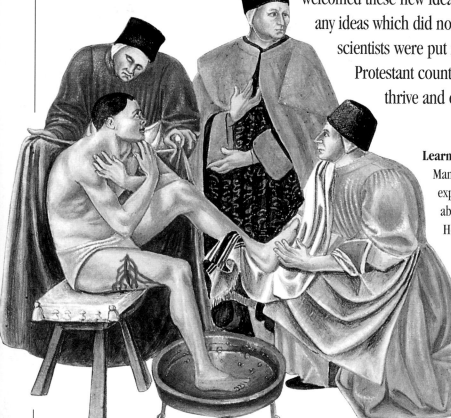

Doctors treating illnesses or wounds had centuries of trial and error behind them, but during the Renaissance they could rely on new experiments and data. Andreas Vesalius (1514–64) dissected dozens of human bodies and in 1543 published a book containing pictures and essays on the internal workings of the body.

The Alchemist

This painting by Giovanni Stradano shows the workshop of a leading alchemist. In the foreground a boy (1) grinds chemicals together with a pestle and mortar while an apprentice (2) holds a flask and watches a liquid being distilled from the metal pot into the glass flask (3). Another apprentice (4) heats and stirs a liquid under the supervision of the alchemist himself. To the left, a man (5) uses a screw press to squeeze liquid, probably from fruits or herbs. In the background other assistants (6) heat liquids while others check the stock of chemicals.

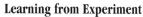

Renaissance Art

The Renaissance was a time of exceptional vitality in the arts. An extraordinary number of masterpieces – in painting, sculpture, metalworking and architecture – were produced. Some of the greatest artists lived at this time, including Brunelleschi, Masaccio, Michelangelo, Leonardo da Vinci, Raphael and Titian in Italy; Dürer, Holbein and Cranach in Germany; and Van Eyck and Memling in Flanders. The new atmosphere of freedom of ideas at the time encouraged artists to explore new techniques. At the same time the sudden boom in wealth encouraged many merchants, noblemen and town councils to spend money on works of art. Building on the work of a number of 14th-century artists, painters learned how to show perspective. Sculptors studied statues from ancient Rome and Greece, learning how to carve stone in new ways to show movement and drama. Metalworkers were eager to catch up and developed a method of casting large bronze figures, up to 33 feet tall. From Italy these new techniques and ideas spread out across all of Europe. Soon artists were working in the new style, producing even more ideas and skills. By about 1600, however, the old freedoms began to be lost. Merchants and noblemen no longer had as much money to spend on art, and town councils preferred to use their taxes to pay for strong walls and armies to protect themselves.

The artist's workshop

During the Renaissance the finest painters, sculptors, goldsmiths and other artists each had their own workshop. The artist accepted commissions from the Church, the nobility or wealthy merchants. For an important client, the artist would do most of the work himself, but other works would be a team effort by the workers in the studio. Young boys would join the studio at the age of about seven, when they would mix paints, sharpen chisels and undertake other mundane tasks. By the age of about 13 the boys became pupil artists, learning from the master artist. Within a few years they would be painting backgrounds or trees, while the master painted the main figures and foregrounds. At the age of 18 the young artist's training would be complete. He might stay in the studio to work on minor pieces, but if he was good enough he might set up his own studio.

In 1488 the 13-year-old Michelangelo Buonarroti (1475–1564) joined the studio of Florentine artist Domenico Ghirlandaio (1449–94). After just two years, the boy was spotted by the ruler of Florence, Lorenzo the Magnificent, who encouraged him to work in stone. Michelangelo went on to become one of the greatest sculptors and fresco painters of all time.

The Trinity

Masaccio's *Trinity*, in the basilica of Santa Maria Novella in Florence, provoked wonder when it was first unveiled in 1427. It shows God the Father (1) supporting his son's cross (2) and a dove (3), symbolizing the Holy Ghost. St. John (4) and the Virgin (5) are shown standing below this Holy Trinity, while the two patrons (6) who commissioned the work kneel just outside the painted architectural setting. This fresco is one of the most amazing studies in perspective in western European painting. In 1550, the artist and historian Vasari wrote: "a barrel-vaulted ceiling, drawn in perspective and divided into square compartments containing rosettes, foreshortened so skillfully that it seems to pierce the wall."

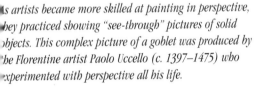

As artists became more skilled at painting in perspective, they practiced showing "see-through" pictures of solid objects. This complex picture of a goblet was produced by the Florentine artist Paolo Uccello (c. 1397–1475) who experimented with perspective all his life.

The rediscovery of perspective

One of the most significant developments of Renaissance art was the rediscovery of perspective, making objects in the distance look as if they really are far away. The ancient Romans left a few frescoes which showed this feature, but in medieval times paintings rarely showed real scenes. Instead pictures showed saints and holy figures on flat backgrounds of a single color. The first artist to break this tradition was the Florentine Giotto di Bondone (c. 1266–1337). He removed unnecessary features, such as gilding, and painted fields or buildings behind the main figures. He painted distant objects smaller than foreground objects, but did not manage to develop perspective. It was another hundred years before Masaccio realized that for a picture to look realistic all horizontal lines leading away from the viewer had to appear to meet at a point on the distant horizon, the "vanishing point." Once this and other key developments had been perfected, artists could paint almost any scene, real or imagined, as if it really existed. It became fashionable to paint a window with a view so realistic that people were fooled into thinking they could look out.

New Worlds

In 1400 Europeans knew little about what lay beyond Europe and the Near East. Although a few scholars knew the world was round, many believed it was flat. Some travelers had visited India or China and heard stories about Japan and the "Spice islands" (the Molaccas, now part of Indonesia), but they knew nothing about the Americas, Australia, the Pacific or most of Africa. In 1415 Prince Henry of Portugal set up a school for navigators and sent his sailors south along the west coast of Africa. They found new territories and rich trading opportunities. Before long other nations were exploring new areas, hoping to make as much money from trade or looting as the Portuguese. In 1492 Christopher Columbus landed in the Americas while trying to sail west to China. By about 1550 Europeans were sailing all over the globe, and before long they began setting up trading stations in, or taking over, the lands they discovered.

The figure shown here is using a cross-staff. By lining up the bottom edges of the two crosspieces with the horizon and the two upper edges with a star, a navigator could discover the angle at which the object lay above the horizon. By consulting a series of tables, the approximate distance from the equator could be found.

The caravel

Caravels were small merchant ship developed in the western Mediterranea during the 14th and 15th centuries. Ear caravels had triangular lateen sails, ide. for beating against a wind. Later version had square rigging on the first two mas to make them better suited for lon voyages with the wind. They were the firs ships to have a rudder, not a steerin oar, and lacked unwieldy high forecastles and sterncastles. Togethe with the large hold in which to stor provisions, these features made carave ideal for long voyages of exploration

Christopher Columbus

Christopher Columbus, an experienced sailor and navigator, believed that the world was round and that if he sailed westward across the Atlantic he would reach Japan and China. Many people thought he was crazy but some, including the king and queen of Spain, who financed his expedition in 1492, believed him. Columbus landed in the present-day West Indies, although he believed that he had reached the coast of China. Although he made three more journeys to America, he died firmly convinced that he had discovered the western sea route to the Far East.

Vasco da Gama

Tempted by the vast riches to be gained by trading with India, the Portuguese sailor Vasco da Gama (c. 1460–1524) left Lisbon in 1497. The Arabs who controlled the trade between India and Europe tried to stop him, but da Gama reached Calicut in May 1498. His voyage showed a profit of 600% and led to many other trading missions. In 1502 da Gama retired from the sea to enjoy the enormous wealth he had gained.

Hernando Cortés

Hernando Cortés (1485–1547) landed on the coast of Mexico with 550 men and 17 horses to found a new colony in 1518. He discovered the Aztec Empire, the ruler of which, Montezuma, mistook Cortés for a god. Cortés took over the Aztec Empire, ruling through Montezuma. But a rebellion by the Aztecs led to fighting and Cortés suffered dreadful losses before destroying the Aztec capital in 1521 and taking over as military governor on behalf of the King of Spain.

Francisco Pizarro

In 1531 the Spaniard Francisco Pizarro (c. 1475–1541) left Mexico with 183 men to investigate stories of a gold-rich kingdom to the south. He found the Inca Empire in the middle of a civil war and used this situation to kill the Inca emperor and install a puppet ruler. Pizarro and his men looted tons of gold and silver from the Incas, but then faced years of warfare as the Incas rose in rebellion. Pizarro was murdered by a fellow Spaniard before he could enjoy the fruits of his conquest.

Ferdinand Magellan

In 1519, the Portuguese navigator Ferdinand Magellan (c. 1480–1521) set out with a fleet of five ships to find a western route to the Spice islands. In August 1520 he sailed into the Pacific through the straits which now bear his name. Because he miscalculated the width of the Pacific Ocean, Magellan and his men almost died of starvation and scurvy before reaching the Philippines in March 1521. Magellan and most of his men were killed in a local war, but the *Vittoria*, commanded by Juan del Cano, returned to Spain in July 1522. The 38 survivors of the 270 men who had set out had completed the first voyage around the world.

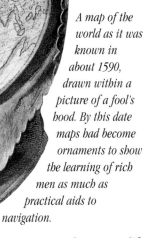

The technology of exploration

The great voyages of exploration were possible because several crucial inventions came together in the late 15th century. The rudder and sailing rig of the caravels made long voyages safer, while improvements in navigation made it possible for captains to know where they were, even out of sight of land. Air-tight wooden barrels made it possible to store food and water for weeks without rotting.

…ortable …mpass …unted in a wooden box. Compasses …ve navigators the ability to find north …a cloudy night for the first time.

A map of the world as it was known in about 1590, drawn within a picture of a fool's hood. By this date maps had become ornaments to show the learning of rich men as much as practical aids to navigation.

The Three Caravels

This 15th-century painting by Spanish artist Monleon shows Columbus's three ships setting out to America on August 3, 1492. Columbus journeyed aboard the flagship *Santa Maria* (1). The other boats were the *Niña* (2) and the *Pinta* (3).

Navigation

During the 15th century many technical advances made navigating a science rather than an art. The cross-staff measured the angle of a star above the horizon to fix the distance from the horizon at night. The later backstaff, a similar arrangement of wooden pieces, relied on the sun casting a shadow during the day. The difficulty of using these instruments on a ship's rolling deck made them imprecise instruments, but a good navigator could fix the north-south position of his ship to within about 30 miles. Navigators could calculate the distance traveled east to west by dead reckoning. This involved measuring the speed of the ship and multiplying by the time sailed. Because this method did not take account of tides or currents it was very inaccurate and navigators could be hundreds of miles out in their results.

A dangerous life

Being a sailor on a long voyage was a dangerous occupation. The small ships of the time were easily shipwrecked or damaged by storms. Food often went rotten, leading to starvation, and scurvy caused by a lack of vitamins was common. On the other hand the rewards could be enormous. Some sailors returned from a single voyage rich for life.

Index

The publishers would like to thank the following picture libraries and photographers for permission to reproduce their photos:

Cover: Benozzo Gozzoli, *The Procession of the Magi*, Florence, Palazzo Medici-Riccardi (Index-Orsi Battaglini, Florence)

6–7 Scala Group, Florence; 8–9 The Bridgeman Art Library / Overseas; 11 The Bridgeman Art Library / Overseas; 12 Scala Group, Florence; 13 Cussac, Musées Royaux des Beaux-Arts de Belgique; 16–17 Santa Maria della Scala, Siena / Foto3-Fabio Lensini, Siena; 21 The Bridgeman Art Library / Overseas; 22 Shakespeare Birthplace Trust, Stratford-upon-Avon; 24–25 Scala Group, Florence; 26 J.-L. Bulloz, Istituto Geografico De Agostini; 29 Bildarchiv Preussischer Kulturbesitz, Berlin; 31 Scala Group, Florence; 33 Scala Group, Florence; 35 Museo Naval, Madrid.